So, You Had a Tough Week, Huh?

Experiencing the Mysteries of God's Leading

A True Story

By Rick Stem

DEDICATION

I dedicate this book to my brother, Tim, who died on Sunday morning of July 10, 2022. He will be missed.

ABOUT THE AUTHOR

Rick was born and raised in Centre County, Pennsylvania. He grew up on the dairy and beef farms his father worked. As a young man, he accepted Jesus Christ as his Lord and Savior and accepted God's calling into the ministry.

Rick graduated from Valley Forge Christian College with a bachelor's degree in Bible. He has served in full-time ministry as a pastor and a pastor of evangelism. He has served in full-time law enforcement as a deputy sheriff and as a police officer. While working in law enforcement, Rick served as a police k-9 handler and trained other police k-9 dog/handler teams as well.

Rick has trained dogs professionally for dog owners for over forty years. Because of his experience in the above, Rick published his first book in 2006 entitled *Seeing God Through The Eyes Of A Dog Trainer.* In 2015 Rick Published his second book entitled *The Intercessor.* In 2021 Rick published his third book entitled *Servants Of The Most High God-Bring My Children Home.*

Rick is a licensed minister with the South Carolina District of the Assemblies of God.

CONTENTS

INTRODUCTION

Let me say right from the beginning that this is a true story. It is a story of a trip my wife, Lois, and I recently made to Pennsylvania. I am sure you are already asking yourself, "What is so important that I had to write a story about a trip to Pennsylvania?"

As Christian believers we often do things thinking all the time that it is our endeavors we are doing and for our purposes. But as endeavors turn out, we sometimes experience things that turn out differently than we planned and we cannot figure out why. Whether we realize it or not we come to experience that God has His own plans for His own purposes and we are a part of that plan and that purpose. Such was the case with our trip.

I have lived the Pentecostal Christian life for over forty-seven years now. Lois has lived the Pentecostal Christian life for even longer than me even though she is younger than me. Lois grew up in a Pentecostal Christian home and I was saved from a life of sin at the age of nineteen. God brought us together at Bible college as we were both studying for ministry.

I became a credentialed minister with the Assemblies of God in 1981. Lois and I have experienced life in the Spirit and we both have taught on the person and work of the Holy Spirit, including the Pentecostal distinctive of speaking in other tongues. We both have lived by faith in God and over the years God has grown our faith in Him. If you, the reader, are a Christian believer you can identify with us. But on this trip God tested our faith, and not just our faith, but our patience as well.

If you are a reader who has not yet come into a personal relationship with God through faith in His Son, Jesus Christ, I hope this book will encourage you to do so. Faith in God is an absolute necessity in coming into a personal relationship with God. The author of Hebrews states in Hebrews 11:6, "And without faith it is impossible to please God, because anyone who comes to Him must believe that He exists and that He rewards those who earnestly seek Him."

As an author, I write not only to the Christian believer but also to the non-believer who has not yet come to saving faith in God and His Son, Jesus Christ. For the reader who has not yet come to faith in God and His Son, Jesus Christ, you may be asking yourself, "How does one get this faith?" I encourage you with the words of the Apostle Paul in Romans 10:17, "Consequently, faith comes from hearing the message, and the message is heard through the word of Christ." This is why I share the scriptures whenever I write.

I mentioned that God tested our faith but He also tested our patience as well. The International Standard Bible Encyclopedia defines patience as "implies suffering, enduring or waiting, as a determination of the will and not simply under necessity. As such it is an essential Christian virtue to the exercise of which there are many exhortations. We need to "wait patiently" for God, to endure uncomplainingly the various forms of sufferings, wrongs and evils that we meet with, and to bear patiently injustices which we cannot remedy and provocations we cannot remove."

To the Christian believer who either lacks patience or desires to develop their patience the Apostle James declares in James 1:2-4, "Consider it pure joy, my brothers, whenever you face trials of many kinds, because you know that the testing of your faith develops perseverance. Perseverance must finish its work so that you may be mature and complete, not lacking anything."

After living the Pentecostal Christian life and serving God in the ministry for these many years, I suppose that God had more refining work to do in both Lois's and my life. As Christian believers we know that this developmental work takes place through the ministry of the Holy Spirit who indwells the life of every Christian believer.

Every Christian believer experiences spiritual trials throughout their life. Most Christian believers probably do not ask God for the trials of life to come their way. But then we do not need to, because God is going to do that for us. And the trials God brings our way are usually as a surprise to us—we did not see them coming.

The positive way for the Christian believer to look at the trials of life which God uses to strengthen our faith and develop our patience is by

9

embracing the words of the Apostle Paul in Romans 8:28-30, "And we know that in all things God works for the good of those who love Him, who have been called according to His purpose. For those God foreknew He also predestined to be conformed to the likeness of His Son; that He might be the firstborn among many brothers. And those He predestined, He also called; those He called, He also justified; those He justified, He also glorified."

In closing, as you read this book, I pray that you will be ministered unto, blessed, encouraged and may it bring glory to God the Father and His Son, Jesus Christ.

CHAPTER ONE

A Clarion Call

It had been approximately three- and one-half years since I last saw my brother, Tim, and that was in October 2018 at my dad's memorial service. From time to time we would talk on the phone but there just hadn't been a convenient time for me to drive the over twelve-hour drive and over seven hundred and fifty miles to go see him.

But late afternoon of Monday, May 9, 2022, I received a text from Tim's daughter, Leslie, that Tim was admitted into a hospital in Pennsylvania. When I enquired of her as to the reason he was in the hospital she informed me it was the results of an irreversible liver disease. I immediately told her that I would pray for him. I also texted prayer partners (brothers and sisters in the body of Christ) to join me in intercessory prayer for Tim.

My brother, Tim, is a Christian brother in the Lord as well as my natural brother in the flesh. Many years ago, Tim, like every Christian believer, repented of his sins and asked Jesus to forgive him of his sins and cleanse him of his sins. The Apostle Paul says in Romans 3:23, "for all have sinned and fall short of the glory of God." But the Apostle John states in 1 John 1:9, "If we confess our sins, He is faithful and just and will forgive us our sins and purify us from all unrighteousness."

My prayer partners and I began to pray for God to heal Tim of this deadly disease. My prayer partners are Christian believers who believe in the truth of God's word. We believe that according to Isaiah 53:5, there is physical healing for the person who puts saving faith in God and His Son, Jesus Christ. Listen to the powerful statement God spoke through His servant, the prophet Isaiah. Isaiah 53:5, "But He was pierced for our transgressions, He was crushed for our iniquities; the punishment that brought us peace was upon Him and by His wounds we are healed. We believe that Jesus not only died for our sins but for our physical healing as well.

The next morning, Tuesday, May 10, 2022, I called Tim and talked with him on the phone. I told Tim, "God is not just with you in this situation, but God is going to lead you through this situation." I went on to say, "Tim, God is not just going to lead you down this path of dealing with your physical infirmity but, He is going to lead your whole family down this path; revealing Himself to you and your family of His presence within you and the work He is going to do in your life, both physically and spiritually."

I began calling Tim on a daily basis both morning and evening. In the morning calls, I would ask Tim what he was expecting for the day and I would try to encourage him, and I always ended the call with prayer. The evening calls would consist of my asking Tim what went on in his day as well as trying to give him words of encouragement. Each evening call always ended with my praying for him.

There were up and down days for Tim during his stay at the hospital and I knew he was experiencing physical suffering which can affect one emotionally and for the Christian believer, spiritually as well. The Psalmist speaks encouraging words in Psalm 46:1, "God is our refuge and strength, an ever-present help in trouble." One of my favorite verses of scripture is Psalm 91:14, "Because He loves me," says the Lord, "I will rescue him. I will protect him, for he acknowledges my name."

After a few weeks in the hospital which I'm sure seemed like a long time to Tim, the day came when Tim went home. I didn't call Tim that day because I knew he would be busy with all he needed to do in going home. Tim had a very special need as a result of his liver disease. That need was oxygen, and lots of it. Tim was consuming fifteen units of oxygen because of damage to his lungs.

My prayer partners and I were praising God for Tim finally being able to go back home. Tim surely was glad for the opportunity. Most patients in the hospital are probably most thankful to go back home after a stay in the hospital, even if it's a short stay. My prayer partners and I were continuing to pray for Tim's healing.

As Christian believers we can pray to God and ask for that which is beyond man's abilities no matter what our need is. In Jeremiah 32:27 God Himself states, "I am the Lord, the God of all mankind. Is anything too hard for me?" Jesus once told His disciples that nothing is impossible to God because God has the power to do what man cannot do. Luke 18:27, "Jesus replied, "What is impossible with men is possible with God."

I know that many of you reading these words right now are probably asking the question, "If nothing is impossible with God then why does He not heal everyone and instead lets some people die?" God declares in Isaiah 55:8-9, "For my thoughts are not your thoughts, neither are your ways my ways;' declares the Lord. As the heavens are higher than the earth, so are my ways higher than your ways and my thoughts are higher than your thoughts."

As Christian believers we place confidence in God knowing that He can do all things including the healing of my brother, Tim. But as I stated in the introduction to the book, God has His own plans and purposes for our lives. Again, I remind you of the Apostle Paul's words in Romans 8:28, "And we know that in all things God works for the good of those who love Him, who have been called according to His purpose." As Christian believers we can trust in God and His word regardless of our situation.

On Saturday, June 7, 2022, I received a "clarion call" from God. Approaching 7:30 pm I called my mom to see how Tim was doing. I knew she would have been at his home the day before to welcome him home and I assumed she had seen him earlier on this day. My mom told me to call Tim.

"Call Tim, he wants you to call him," she said to me.

A few minutes later I called Tim and began talking with him as I did while he was in the hospital. After a few minutes of conversation Tim said to me, "Well, I may as well tell you, the doctors have told me there's nothing they can do for me and they have placed me under hospice care." Now I can only imagine receiving a statement like that from the doctors. Receiving such a statement could quickly sink one's spirit into hopelessness and despair.

But, because we as Christian believers have put our saving faith in God and His Son, Jesus Christ, we can look at such news with a different perspective than how non-Christians do. Because when an individual comes to faith in Jesus Christ, God, by His Holy Spirit, comes into their life to live within them. The Apostle Paul speaks of the results of our personal relationship we have with God and His Son, Jesus Christ. 1 Corinthians 6:19-20, "Do you not know that your body is a temple of the Holy

Spirit, who is in you, whom you have received from God? You are not your own; you were bought at a price. Therefore, honor God with your body."

Back to the "clarion call." The Oxford Language Dictionary defines clarion call as "a strongly expressed demand or request for action." I did not know at the time of receiving this call that it was God calling me, but eventually I did. God used my brother's statement to me, "The doctors told me that there's nothing they can do for me and that they are placing me under hospice care."

Immediately I began to do something I had not done for over three and one half years, make a trip to go and see Tim. I conducted Sunday morning church service and then prepared to leave early Monday morning because it was going to be a long drive. God used my brother's statement to move me into immediate action. Little did I know that God's "clarion call" would have a literal fulfillment.

CHAPTER TWO

GPS for the Christian Believer

GPS is short for Global Positioning System. In the United States the Federal Aviation Administration (FAA) describes how GPS is utilized: "Satellite Navigation is based on a global network of satellites that transmit radio signals from medium earth orbit. Users of Satellite Navigation are most familiar with the 31 Global Positioning System (GPS) satellites developed and operated by the United States." Make no mistake, the use of GPS in traveling can get you where you want to go even if you don't use a map. Just put in an address and you are on your way.

Early Monday morning, June 6, 2022, Lois and I packed up our 2015 Dodge Grand Caravan with clothes and such as we would need on our trip. Because my son, Abe, was taking his family out of town this same week we took our female German Shepherd and two female Chihuahuas along with us. Lois and I have been involved with dogs all our lives so it wasn't a problem from our perspective. Having been involved in the dog show business for a number of years prepared us for this trip with the dogs.

I had planned a pretty simple itinerary for our trip with plans of returning home by the upcoming Saturday. Today's itinerary consisted of driving from Beaufort, South Carolina all the way to Bellefonte, Pennsylvania. Google estimated the trip to take just over twelve hours and the drive to be over seven hundred-fifty miles. Of course, this was with NO complications of any kind.

It was approximately 6:15 am when we left home. Surely, I could expect us to make it to Bellefonte, Pennsylvania before 7:00 pm and have plenty of time to spare before it became dark. Hey, I might even get in a quick visit with my brother, Tim. That would be great, so I thought.

Our route of travel was fairly simple. We would drive straight up I-95 to the 495 Beltway just past Springfield, Virginia. By the way, I forgot to welcome you, the reader, on our trip. I am glad you can travel along with us in your reading. We only made stops when we needed gas, and gas was not cheap. The price of gas was cheaper in Beaufort and it continued to rise the further north we went. The only other times we stopped was for bathroom breaks for us and the dogs.

I must say that the weather was nice our entire trip. I drove the majority of Monday's trip. I didn't need GPS while driving on I-95 as I was very much familiar with the route, having driven it many times before. So far, the trip was going pretty smoothly. But as we approached the 495 Beltway, it was GPS time. I was not sure how I was going to enter Pennsylvania from the 495 Beltway.

The GPS was leading us, Lois was playing the role of navigator, and I was doing the driving. It reminded me of living the Christian life. The Christian believer lives life not just by faith but also by walking in the Spirit. The Apostle Paul exhorts the Christian believer to walk in the Spirit. Galatians 5:16, "So I say, live by the Spirit, and you will not gratify the desires of the sinful nature." The Apostle Paul gives the reason why we can and must live in the Spirit. Galatians 5:24-25, "Those who belong to Christ Jesus have crucified the sinful nature with its passions and desires. Since we live by the Spirit, let us keep in step with the Spirit."

The GPS continued to guide us towards our destination of Bellefonte, Pennsylvania, though at times I doubted its correctness because I didn't know where I was. We had only the GPS (does one really need anything more?) and no map. The indwelling Holy Spirit is the spiritual GPS for the Christian believer. But God also provides us with a map. The Psalmist says in Psalm 119:105, "Your word is a lamp to my feet and a light for my path."

Again, sad to say, and I am confessing, I questioned the truthfulness of the route the GPS was leading us because I was in unfamiliar territory. If you are a reader who has not put faith in God and His Son, Jesus Christ, and you are asking the question, "How can I know the Bible is the truth?" Jesus Himself once told His disciples that He is the truth. John 14:6, "Jesus answered, "I am the way and the truth and the life. No one comes to the Father but through me.""

But Jesus continued to speak on the truth of the Bible. John 17:17, "Sanctify them by the truth; your word is truth." And to guide the Christian believer the right way to live, God supplies us with His spiritual GPS, the Holy Spirit. John 16:13, "But when He, the Spirit of truth, comes, He will guide you into all truth. He will not speak on His own; He will speak only what He hears, and He will tell you what is yet to come. The Christian believer can put all confidence in this with no doubting.

As we were approaching the entrance to the state of Pennsylvania, the GPS had a route selected for us to go which I thought would take me towards familiar territory. But all of a sudden, the exit to the established route was upon us and I could not switch from the middle lane to the right lane because a large truck was in the right lane, preventing me from getting over in the right lane to exit onto the established route. I missed the exit!

The GPS led us from the state of Maryland into the state of Pennsylvania but into an area I did not know. If you are familiar with the use of GPS you know it will reposition itself and continue leading you towards your destination whether you are familiar with the area or not. We eventually went through a small town called Greencastle that led us into beautiful Pennsylvania farmland on both sides of the road as we traveled from one side of a valley to the other. I was reminded of growing up on the Pennsylvania dairy farms my dad worked. It was a very rewarding part of the trip.

After traveling through the farmland, the GPS led us into a remote wooded area that went for miles and seemingly forever. This was to be the worst part of the day's trip for me. We were driving on a road that had no or few homes along it and to make things worse we had no cell phone coverage. By the way, the longer we drove this route daylight was slowly fading away.

For the second time this day, I didn't know where I was. In fact, I told Lois, "I feel lost, and I don't like feeling lost!" I also told her, "I do not want to be out here in the middle of nowhere in the dark!" With those two statements I thought of those who are spiritually lost, not knowing God or His Son, Jesus Christ. Spiritually these people don't know where they are. They have no spiritual guidance system, no spiritual map, and they don't know who to call if in need of help.

But Lois, my navigator, was assuring me we were headed towards a major road that I was familiar with. As it was getting dark we stopped at a convenient store (if you can believe there was one) and Lois took over the driving. As you can guess, we weren't going to arrive at our destination at the time I had originally intended. We finally made it to

Bellefonte approximately 9:30 pm with most everything closed or closing. At about 10:30 pm with the permission of a convenience store manager we spent the night sleeping in our van in the parking lot of a 24-hour store.

Everything didn't go smoothly or as planned on this first day of our trip. But God did get us to our destination. We had many Christian brothers and sisters praying for us. God was faithful to those praying and He was faithful to Lois and I. We praised Him for being with us through the entire day. But God is faithful to those who put their faith in Him. Tomorrow would bring our visits to my brother.

CHAPTER THREE

A Reunion Between Two Brothers

Having spent the night in our van at the 24-hour convenience store Lois and I were up early. We weren't the only ones who were up early. It was Tuesday morning of June 7, 2022, and drivers from the area were stopping at the convenience store to purchase gas, coffee and other breakfast products on their way to work. I am usually an early riser though Lois is not quite so. But even if I wasn't, the noise made by the incoming shoppers would have probably woken me anyway.

Today's agenda was simple. We were going to visit my brother, Tim, at his home. So, after taking care of our dogs, Lois and I drove to visit my mom who lives approximately five miles past my brother. And for sure she is an early riser. The many years of life on the farm, though almost an eternity in the past, yet seemed to stay with her.

Besides, I didn't want to interrupt my brother's morning in case it took him awhile to get his day started.

The last time I saw my mom, Barbara, was the same time I last saw my brother, Tim. It was three-and one-half years ago at my dad's memorial service in October 2018. Upon first seeing my mom I gave her a hug and it was then that I noticed her looking older than the last time I saw her. But that is the natural process of life. Everyone experiences it.

Growing old and dying is a result of Adam and Eve's disobedience and sin. Genesis 2:15-17, "The Lord God took the man and put him in the Garden of Eden to work it and take care of it. And the Lord God commanded the man, "You are free to eat from any tree in the garden; but you must not eat from the tree of the knowledge of good and evil, for when you eat of it you will surely die."

When Adam and Eve sinned against God, God was true to His word. God cursed everything: the serpent, Satan, the woman, the ground, and man. To Adam, representing mankind, God cursed him with the promise of spiritual death and physical death. Genesis 3:19, "By the sweat of your brow you will eat your food until you return to the ground, since from it you were taken, for dust you are and to dust you will return." As we live, we grow older and that is just the way it is. There is no stopping the natural process of growing older. And eventually we all die.

I saw my mom's new apartment that she recently moved into. A small and cozy one bedroom apartment that supplied all the daily amenities she needed to live. It was extremely well kept reflecting on her desire for cleanliness and tidiness. And she was allowed to have her dog which Lois and I met; a black Miniature Pinscher named Missy. My mom has always been a dog person because my dad was always a dog person. And as you already know, I have always been a dog person as well.

Our visit with my mom was not a lengthy one. Lois and I then drove to my brother's house with my mom following in her own car. I wasn't sure what to expect upon seeing my brother. Tim is only a year and a half younger than me. Our relationship growing up was generally good, except for a couple of rock fights while growing up on the farm. My grandmother (my mom's mom) used to dress us alike whenever she took us with her to certain important events.

Tim was an excellent baseball player and also became an excellent wrestler. After high school Tim joined the local Army National Guard Unit in Bellefonte where he served a career as an outstanding part-time soldier. Tim got married and even as I write this book, he is going on his 43rd wedding anniversary with his wife, Julie. Tim worked a maintenance career with a local restaurant in State College, Pennsylvania. And Tim has been a committed church goer all his married life. Tim and Julie have been long time members of the United Methodist Church of Howard, Pennsylvania, where he lives.

I say these things to reflect on Tim's character of being committed, dedicated, persevering and in a way, victorious to what his life consisted of. A lot of people do not have that type of record in life. And even now as Tim suffers the liver disease in his body and its results, he continues to reflect on the above-mentioned character qualities. But one character trait that is now seen in Tim is his Godly virtue of faith in God. But not just his faith in God, but his personal relationship with God.

Tim, as a Christian believer, reflects the indwelling presence of the Holy Spirit and His work in Tim's life. As Tim suffers with his physical infirmity yet he reflects his life in the Spirit. He reflects the words of the Apostle Paul in 2 Corinthians 4:16, "Therefore we do not lose heart. Though outwardly we are wasting away, yet inwardly we are being renewed day by day."

Because of the presence of God's Holy Spirit at work in Tim's life he reflects the words of King David in Psalm 23:4, "Even though I walk through the valley of the shadow of death, I will fear no evil, for You are with me; your rod and your staff, they comfort me." For anyone facing the end of life, they can be encouraged by seeing the results of the Holy Spirit's work in Tim's life. God's Holy Spirit has been preparing him to leave this life to enter the heavenly life in the presence of God, his heavenly Father, and his Lord and Savior, Jesus Christ.

Even before seeing Tim, I had been placing full confidence in the Holy Spirit bringing this reflection about in Tim's life. And sure enough, as I met with Tim. I could see the results of the presence and ministry of the Holy Spirit in Tim's life. As a pastor I personally enjoy seeing the workings of the Holy Spirit in a Christian believer's life.

The Apostle Paul describes it as the fruit of the Spirit in Galatians 5:22, "But the fruit of the Spirit is love, joy, peace, patience, kindness, goodness, faithfulness, gentleness and self-control. Against such things there is no law."

It was good to see my brother, Tim, again. There were Tim, and his wife, Julie, his daughter, Leslie, my mom, Lois, and I sitting together in his living room. After we talked for a while, we had communion consisting of crackers and juice. I wanted to do communion together so that despite all of our recognition of Tim's condition which he deals with daily, that we could shift our attention to Jesus.

The Apostle Paul says in 1 Corinthians 11:23-25, "For I received from the Lord what I passed on to you: The Lord Jesus, on the night He was betrayed, took bread, and when He had given thanks, He broke it and said, "This is my body, which is for you; do this in remembrance of me." In the same way, after supper He took the cup, saying, "This cup is the new covenant in my blood; do this, in remembrance of me." For whenever you eat this bread and drink this cup, you proclaim the Lord's death until He comes."

When the hospice nurse came to minister to Tim, my mom went home and Lois and I went to lunch. We returned to Tim's house for an afternoon visit in which we talked about an upcoming doctor's appointment Tim was to have with a liver transplant team at a hospital in Philadelphia on Monday, June 20, 2022. Hope was in the air. Conversation with Tim was challenging because of the oxygen mask that he wore. His oxygen hose was connected to two large oxygen machines that continually gave Tim the oxygen he needed. But the two visits went well and our reunion together was good.

I made plans to come back the next day and visit Tim. Lois and I left and rented a cabin at a KOA Campground for the night which was not far from Tim's home. A TV to watch, a bed to sleep in, and looking toward the opportunity of another visit with my brother brought an end to the day. And as Christian believers Lois and I thanked God for His blessings upon us this day.

CHAPTER FOUR

And The Greatest of These Is Love

1 Corinthians 13:1-13, "If I speak in the tongues of men and of angels, but have not love, I am only a resounding gong or a clanging cymbal. If I have the gift of prophecy and can fathom all mysteries and all knowledge, and if I have a faith that can move mountains, but have not love, I am nothing. If I give all I possess to the poor and surrender my body to the flames, but have not love, I am nothing.

Love is patient, love is kind. It does not envy, it does not boast, it is not proud. It is not rude, it is not self-seeking, it is not easily angered, it keeps no record of wrongs. Love does not delight in evil but rejoices with the truth. It always protects, always trusts, always hopes, always perseveres.

Love never fails. But where there are prophecies, they will cease; where there are tongues, they will be stilled; where there is knowledge, it will pass away. For we know in part and we prophesy in part, but when perfection comes, the imperfect disappears. When I was a child, I acted like a child, I talked like a child, I reasoned like a child. When I became a man, I put childish ways behind me. Now we see but a poor reflection as in a mirror; then we shall see face to face. Now I know in part; then I shall know fully, even as I am fully known.

And now these three remain: faith, hope, and love. But the greatest of these is love."

It was the morning of Wednesday, June 8, 2022. After a night's stay at the KOA Campground, we packed our van with what we unpacked the night before, including our dogs. The plan for the day was to visit with my brother again and then continue traveling west on I-80 heading to Lois's mother's house whom she hadn't seen for five years. It was to be a surprise visit. The day's itinerary seemed simple.

We arrived at my brother's house by midmorning. My mom was already there. What we didn't see much of on the day before we surely saw on this day, Tim's cats. Tim has four healthy middle-aged cats. Only three of them were in our midst during our visit. The fourth cat kept herself hidden.

I'm not a cat person. But Tim's one cat, Chip, a silver tiger striped tabby caught my attention. Chip was a friendly and sociable cat without putting on some kind of cat show to get it. He just strolled across the floor in a quiet, majestic type of way, walked over to Tim's chair and jumped up onto Tim's lap. He just lay there absorbing my attention. Chip seemed to show cat loyalty to Tim as well as any dog could. I liked him!

Having been reunited with my brother the day before as well as not knowing if I would see him again, rekindled my love for Tim and my appreciation and respect for him. Through tears I told Tim, "I want you to know that I love you!" Through sobs of tears I next said, "I just can't convey to you how much I love you!" I then went on to say to Tim, still with tears, "Tim, my greatest desire for you is for you to experience fellowship with "The Father" (referring to God, his heavenly Father).

My mom had left earlier and it was just Tim and Julie, and Lois and me. We all had a word of prayer together. Lois held Tim's one hand and I held the other. After we finished praying Tim kept a hold of my hand a few minutes longer before I excused myself. Since Tim had a scheduled doctor's appointment with hospital doctors in Philadelphia on June 20, I thought he had more time ahead of him, so I told Tim, "I'll see you again!" I asked Tim to keep me informed.

Tim said in reply, "I'll call you!"

With that, Lois and I left Tim's house. We now were traveling west on I-80 heading to Ellwood City, Pennsylvania to give a surprise visit to Lois's mother, Beverly. On our way on I-80 later that afternoon I received a phone call from Tim.

Tim said, "I'm going to a hospital in Pittsburgh tonight, they say they can do more for me than the hospital in Philadelphia."

The hope level just got raised.

As we were approaching Ellwood City, once again we had a little difficulty following the GPS to Lois's and my niece's house where we would be spending the next two nights. When we did arrive there, we found it to be a restored two-story house on a knoll at the end of a street. It was very spacious with a huge fenced back yard which was very beneficial to our dogs. But it had one negative. We had no cell phone coverage there. To me, having no ability to communicate is almost as bad as not knowing where I am.

Upon securing our dogs in our niece's house we drove to Lois's mother's house to surprise her mother. When Lois walked into her mother's house her mother was pleasantly surprised. We had a time of visiting over supper with Lois's mother, Beverly, Lois's sister, Arloene and her husband, Denni along with our two nephews, Rocco and Saverio, and our niece, Nichole, before going back to Nicole's house for the night.

So far, the trip was pretty much playing out as I had planned. Once again Lois and I thanked God, our heavenly Father, for accomplishing the day's itinerary. Thursday would be a full day of Lois visiting with her mother.

CHAPTER FIVE

I Need a Word, Lord

Thursday morning arrived with sunshine as the sun rose over the horizon. A pretty strong thunderstorm had gone through the area during the night. I did not have the best night's sleep that I would like to have had, but I still didn't hear the storm as it supposedly thundered and poured forth lighting as well as produced strong winds and heavy rains. I really did not see the effects of the storm in the morning where we were staying.

After breakfast and having taken care of our dogs, a daily routine, whether you're traveling or not, we drove to Lois's mother's house in Ellwood City. I knew my brother had been admitted into ICU the night before. Lois's mother lived in a third story condominium, which first thing in the morning I did not feel like climbing. Besides, my brother, Tim, was heavy on my mind and heart. I was also a little tired from not sleeping well the night before. So, I stayed in the van, dozing and praying.

Leslie, Tim's daughter who is a nurse, texted Lois with information she and Tim received from the doctors. Leslie had stated that the doctors were very attentive to them as they performed one test after another on Tim. Remember, the level of hope was raised in everyone caring for Tim.

As a pastor, I am involved continuously in intercessory prayer for others, no matter how great and urgent the prayer request. I pray in faith, believing for God to answer prayer and meet the need, even for serious health conditions such as Tim was suffering. One night when Tim was in the first hospital and having a rough time, I went to God in prayer and said, "Father, I want to intercede for my brother tonight, but I'm "feeling him," and I need your help."

Quickly, God, by His Holy Spirit replied, "I know you are, I was feeling my Son in His suffering." This morning was similar to that night. I once again was "feeling Tim," as I was interceding for him in prayer. I requested help from the Holy Spirit. The Apostle Paul states that the Holy Spirit intercedes for us when we are having a difficult time in prayer.

Romans 8:26-27, In the same way, the Spirit helps us in our weakness. We do not know what we ought to pray for, but the Spirit Himself intercedes for us with groans that words cannot express. And He who searches our hearts knows the mind of the Spirit, because the Spirit intercedes for the saints in accordance with God's will."

I knew this passage of scripture well because I find Romans chapter eight a chapter to go to when facing not just the tough spiritual storms of life, but even when facing the spiritual hurricanes in life. I asked the Holy Spirit for help.

I prayed, "Holy Spirit give me a word of encouragement for my brother, Tim, his daughter, Leslie, and all my prayer partners who I know are interceding in prayer for Tim."

It seemed like a minute later and a passage of scripture came to me. Psalm 91:14-16, "Because he loves me," says the Lord, "I will rescue him; I will protect him for he acknowledges my name. He will call upon me, and I will answer him; I will be with him in trouble, I will deliver him and honor him. With long life will I satisfy him and show him my salvation."

I believe by faith that the Holy Spirit gave me this word. I wrote up the text and then sent it out. I thanked the Holy Spirit for giving me a most encouraging word for Tim and Leslie who were at the hospital and for all those who were praying for Tim.

I then visited with my mother-in-law, Beverly, and Lois's older sister, Arloene, and her husband, Denni. After supper we joined in a word of prayer. Lois and I then went back to our niece's house for the night. God was faithful and got us through another day according to my itinerary schedule. We thanked God for His faithfulness to us. The next morning would bring Lois and I another day of traveling.

CHAPTER SIX

Short Road Again

It was Friday morning, June 10, 2022, and Lois and I and our dogs were on the road again. We had one more person to visit before going back home, my aunt Donna, who lives in Massillon, Ohio. The last time I visited my aunt Donna was in August 2014. My aunt Donna is one of my mom's sisters. By Google she was only two hours away.

We used the GPS as we drove country roads to I-80. From I-80 we drove west into Ohio where Lois and I and our two children, Rebecca and Abe, once lived in the Kent-Ravenna area of Portage County. When I think about it, it was over twenty-nine years ago when we moved from there to South Carolina. It is amazing how fast time moves by.

It was about lunch time when we arrived at my aunt Donna's house. It was good to see her. Through the years I have kept in touch with her by talking on the phone on at least a weekly basis. It reminds me of the Christian believer's relationship with God. God and His Son, Jesus Christ, are in heaven. But because of our having put faith in Jesus Christ, God has come into our lives via His Holy Spirit.

The Apostle Paul describes the Christian believer's relationship with God as a Father and son relationship. Romans 8:15-16, "For you did not receive a spirit that makes you a slave again to fear, but you received the spirit of sonship. And by Him we cry, "Abba, Father." The Spirit Himself testifies with our spirit that we are God's children."

The point I want to make is this: even though I haven't physically seen my aunt Donna for a number of years I still have a relationship with her that is very much alive because of my talking with her on the phone. As Christian believers we have a relationship with God, our heavenly Father whom we have never seen, nor will ever see because He is Spirit. We have our Father-son relationship with God because of our relationship with His Son, Jesus Christ.

As Christian believers we have not seen Him either, but one day we will see Him. We will not only see Him but the Apostle John says we shall be like Him. 1 John 3:2, "Dear friends, now we are children of God, and what we will be has not yet been made known. But we know that when He appears, we shall be like Him, for we shall see Him as He is."

Lois and I spent Friday afternoon visiting with my aunt Donna until the approach of supper time. We then went to a restaurant that served Amish style food. It seemed the place to go if one is in our age category (grandparents). But I must say the food was good.

In Pittsburgh, my brother, Tim, and his daughter, Leslie, had been meeting with doctors from a liver transplant team as well as Tim undergoing various tests. Remember, it was on Tuesday that a liver transplant team of doctors in Philadelphia wanted to meet with Tim on June 20, giving an impression of having a longer road in front of him. This had elevated the hope level for Tim, as well as for family and friends.

It was after Lois and I got back to my aunt Donna's house from the restaurant that Lois received a text from Tim's daughter, Leslie, which stated Tim would be going back home on Saturday morning. I called Leslie and talked with her. She informed me that the doctors had told them that Tim would not be able to survive the liver transplant surgery and that there was nothing they could do for him.

The long road had just become a short road again. According to my itinerary plans Lois and I were scheduled to go back home the next morning via I-77 south. We were just five hours away from Tim. The last thing I told Tim was that "I'll see you again." I did not want the last thing I did with my brother was to lie to him. So, I decided to drive back and see him instead of going back home as I originally planned.

The next morning Lois and I would drive back to Howard, Pennsylvania. We spent the night visiting with my aunt Donna though my thoughts were once again on my brother. For the first time change on the trip was taking place. I was breaking away from my original scheduled plan and schedule and embarking on a new one. Lois and I thanked God for completing the itinerary for this day. A night's sleep lay between us and what lay ahead.

CHAPTER SEVEN

The Mechanic

When it comes to the affairs of life and frankly, anything and everything that goes on in the universe on any given day, the Christian believer can have peace in knowing that God, their heavenly Father, knows everything that happens and is going to happen before it happens because He is God. Isaiah 46:9-10, "Remember the former things, those of long ago; I am God, and there is no other; I am God, and there is none like me. I make known the end from the beginning, from ancient times, what is still to come. I say: My purpose will stand, and I will do all that I please."

Even though God is the creator and sovereign ruler of the universe, yet He is involved in the affairs of every one of His children, whoever they are, and He directs their paths. Psalm 37:23, "The steps of a good man are ordered by the Lord, And He delights in his way." (NKJV) And yet because of His great love for sinful man, God is also involved in the lives of those who have not yet come to Him in faith and received His great salvation through His Son, Jesus Christ. God pursues the unbeliever, sometimes bringing them and His children together so they, the unbeliever, once again can hear the gospel message of salvation.

It was Saturday morning, June 11, 2022. My original plan was to leave my aunt Donna's house and head home on I-77 south to South Carolina. But on Friday evening I was compelled to change my mind and drive back to Howard, Pennsylvania, to visit my brother, Tim, one more time. What compelled me to change my mind was not only Tim going back home from the hospital, but the last thing I told Tim was, "I'll see you again." Truth be spoken, I did not want to lie to Tim.

We were headed eastbound and Lois was driving this part of the trip. About two miles before reaching the exit for Clarion, Pennsylvania, Lois noticed the temperature gauge in the van showing hot, overheating. About one mile later she did an emergency pull off of I-80 at a convenience store with gas which was right off the road. The engine was steaming and clanging. It did not present a good picture. Thankfully we were not stranded way out in the middle of nowhere. But the location gave Lois and I no cell phone coverage. We were STUCK!

We had no mechanical problems with the van during the entire trip, UNTIL NOW. That familiar question many of God's children ask him when finding themselves in a seriously difficult situation came to mind. Why God?

Immediately we realized our need to lean on God because this situation was beyond anything we could do to remedy it. We were borrowing the convenience store clerk's cell phone but we couldn't find help. This was approximately 12:30 pm on a Saturday and we were far from home or anyone we knew.

The woman store clerk who had lent us her cell phone informed us that she had called a particular garage in Clarion and informed them of our situation. Lois called our car insurance company to get roadside assistance. It wasn't long until a mechanic from the garage that the clerk called showed up at our location.

Immediately I introduced Lois and myself to him as I then told him, "I am a pastor from South Carolina and we drove up to Pennsylvania from South Carolina to visit my brother who's under hospice care for liver disease."

The mechanic, Bob, said in reply, "I'm not a God-fearing man but I try to help people out when I can."

Bob soon realized we needed a new radiator. It was bad enough to unexpectedly break down but now we were looking at spending a couple hundred dollars on parts and service that we had not planned for.

Financially, we could only trust Jesus to somehow bless what we had, but I just wanted to get it towed to Bob's garage and hopefully get it fixed before they closed, so Lois and I could continue our travel to Howard to see Tim. Our wait for the tow truck turned out to be longer than we thought it should take to arrive, two-and one-half hours longer.

When the tow truck finally arrived, we found out what took him so long to arrive. He had driven all the way from Pittsburgh to come and tow our van for us. I told the driver that we had three dogs in the van (yes, the windows were down) and I asked if he could give Lois and I a ride to the garage.

The tow truck driver answered, "No one said anything about passengers, besides the front of my truck is all cluttered up."

Seeing a man in his thirties getting gas I briefly told him of our situation and asked him if he could give Lois and I a ride to the garage. He told me that he had just come from there, but he would be glad to take us to the garage. He went on to speak very favorably about them.

The tow truck driver followed us as we drove up the interstate approximately one mile to the exit for Clarion to the garage where Bob, the mechanic, worked. It was 4:15 pm and the sign on the garage read that they closed at 5:00 pm. I intuitively knew our van was not going to get fixed today.
Everything was laying in front of us. Lois and I truly did not know what God was going to do for us.

Worst case scenario we were prepared to sleep in the van another night.

Time seemed to stand still. Lois and I realized for the moment that we were stranded. We couldn't drive anywhere because our van was undrivable. We had no idea what motels were in Clarion and even if we could find one with vacancy, we had three dogs with us. And even if we found a motel that had a vacant room that accepted pets, we had no way of getting there. Are you, the reader, sensing the spot we were in? We were almost stunned that we couldn't think of what we ought to pray for, let alone believe God to do for us.

In the gospel of Matthew Jesus taught his disciples on the subject of prayer. They were to pray to their heavenly Father in a different way than nonbelievers pray. But Jesus also told them a most encouraging statement about God, their heavenly Father, already knowing what they are in need of before they even pray concerning their needs. Matthew 6:6-8, "But when you pray, go into your room, close the door and pray to your Father, who is unseen. Then your Father, who sees what is done in secret, will reward you. And when you pray, do not keep on babbling like pagans, for they think they will be heard because of their many words. Do not be like them, for your Father knows what you need before you ask Him."

The next thing we hear is Bob, the mechanic, telling us what he is going to do for us. He told us that he was giving us a SUV type of vehicle to drive.

This was a vehicle our dogs could travel in. Bob then told us that he had booked a room for us at a motel that would accept our dogs. And on top of that he handed Lois forty dollars in cash. We had not even prayed yet and God was providing for us through this mechanic who earlier told us, "I'm not a God-fearing man but I try to help people out when I can." I'm sure Bob was operating out of the goodness of his fleshly heart but God was working through Him by His Holy Spirit. Either way we were set for the night.

Bob informed us that he would be in his garage in the morning to fix our van and we could expect it to be ready by 11:00 am. Lois and I and our dogs drove to the motel where we settled in for the night. I looked forward to the next morning and getting our van so we could travel to see my brother one more time. Lois and I praised God for His provisions. Christian brothers and sisters were continually praying for us. What a day we had!

CHAPTER EIGHT

Message of Hope

It was Sunday morning, June 12, 2022. Lois and I were not in church as we normally would have been. And though I was not sharing a message in church for the morning, I did have a message to share in the afternoon. On Saturday night I had called my brother, Tim, and told him Lois and I were driving in to see him on our way home (we would take a different route home). I asked Tim if I could share the biblical teachings of what happens at the moment of death for the Christian believer when they die. I suggested to Tim that if his family members knew this information it could give them encouragement whenever he did die. Tim gave me the allowance for it. It would be a message of hope.

Lois and I were at the garage to get our van before 11:00 am. Bob, the mechanic, gave us some bad news. He told us he would need to put a water pump on the van. Bob then called me aside.

Teary eyed, Bob said, "I have a niece in Georgia who just went home from the hospital to die with stage 4 cancer." Bob then said, "She is like a daughter to me but I can't go and see her. But I want you to go and see your brother. I want you to take the vehicle I gave you to use and go see your brother. Feel free to spend the night if you need to."

It was then Lois and I believed by faith that God had brought us and Bob together so that we could be a witness to him. Before Lois and I left to drive to my brother's house I gave Bob a signed copy of my latest book "Servants of The Most High God-Bring My Children Home."

Bob said to me, "I've survived cancer and I've survived a heart attack; I don't even know why I'm here."

In reply I encouraged Bob by saying, "Bob, read the story of Marshal in my book, I think it may help you answer that question."

Lois and I took his offer and we thanked him. Lois drove us and our three dogs the hour and a half drive to Howard to see Tim and his family. All of Tim's family was there including my mom. I thanked them for the opportunity to share with them what the scriptures teach concerning death for the Christian believer. I told everyone that it is truly a message of hope.

I told Tim and his family that whoever believes in Jesus can receive eternal life. John 3:16, "For

God so loved the world that He gave His one and only Son, that whoever believes in Him shall not perish but have eternal life." I then told Tim and his family that Jesus is in heaven right now. Mark 16:19, "After the Lord Jesus had spoken to them, He was taken up into heaven and He sat at the right hand of God." I went on to tell Tim and his family that at the moment of death Tim's spirit (because he is a Christian believer) will depart from his body and the angels of heaven will carry Tim's spirit to heaven. Luke 16:22, "The time came when the beggar died and the angels carried him to Abraham's side. The rich man also died and was buried."

I told them that the angels carrying the spirits of Christian believers to heaven is super quick so that the Apostle Paul describes, that at the time of death is to be present with Jesus. 2 Corinthians 5:8, "We are confident, I say, and would prefer to be away from the body and at home with the Lord." I went on to tell Tim and his family that all the sufferings in this life will be over when we get to heaven. Revelation 21:4, "He will wipe every tear from their eyes. There will be no more death or mourning or crying or pain, for the old order of things has passed away."

I then went on to tell Tim and his family of their opportunity to not only see each other again, but to never be separated again for all eternity. 1 Thessalonians 4:13-18, "Brothers, we do not want you to be ignorant about those who fall asleep, or to grieve like the rest of men, who have no hope. We believe that Jesus died and rose again and so we believe that God will bring with Jesus those who have fallen asleep in him. According to the Lord's own word, we tell you that we who are still alive, who are left till the coming of the Lord, will certainly not precede those who have fallen asleep.

For the Lord Himself will come down from heaven, with a loud command, with the voice of the archangel and with the trumpet call of God, and the dead in Christ will rise first. After that, we who are still alive and are left will be caught up together with them in the clouds to meet the Lord in the air. And so, we will be with the Lord forever. Therefore encourage each other with these words."

I then told Tim and his family that at the rapture and resurrection all Christian believers will get a new and glorified body, just like Jesus when He rose from the dead. It will be a body made for heaven and eternity. It will not have the weaknesses of our present bodies. 1 Corinthians 15:51-53, I declare to you, brothers, that flesh and blood cannot inherit the kingdom of God, nor does the perishable inherit the imperishable. Listen, I tell you a mystery: We will not all sleep, but we will all be changed–in a flash, in the twinkling of an eye, at the last trumpet.

For the trumpet will sound, the dead will be raised imperishable, and we will be changed. For the perishable must clothe itself with the imperishable, and the mortal with immortality." What a message of hope for the Christian believer!

I was thankful for the opportunity Tim gave me to share those most encouraging words with him and his family.

As I sat next to Tim, he presented a picture of someone who trusted God for his salvation as well as where he will spend eternity. I could see the results of God's Holy Spirit having prepared him for the time that eventually befalls every man.

Tim told me, "Mom has a husband in heaven, now she will have a son in heaven."

I told Tim, "You're just going ahead of the rest of us, but eventually we'll all be following, unless the rapture occurs first."

Lois and I said our good-byes and then left. I called Bob, the mechanic, to tell him we would be driving back to Clarion to get our van. Bob then gave me more bad news concerning my van,

"Your van has a blown head gasket," he said.

"'How much does that cost to fix?" I asked.

"About as much as it costs to put another engine in it," replied Bob.

I then knew Lois and I were not leaving Clarion tonight. Lois called the motel where we stayed Saturday night to book a room but the motel informed her all rooms were taken, there were no vacancies.

At Leslie's (Tim's daughter) invitation Lois and I and our dogs spent the night at Leslie and her husband Rex's house on Sunday night. Lois and I thanked God for a place to spend the night with our dogs. Come Monday morning we would drive to

Clarion and see if we could find the way to go home. The clarion call had been literally fulfilled. Lois and I were stranded in Clarion, Pennsylvania. Two questions presented themselves to us. How would we get home and when would we get home?"

CHAPTER NINE

Monday, A Day of Uncertainties

In the 1960's there was a popular song sung on American radio stations nationwide. The song was about the first day of the American work week–Monday, and the uncertainties that day presented. On Monday morning, June 13, 2022, Lois and I left Leslie and Rex's house to drive the hour and a half drive back to Clarion. The morning was presenting us with various uncertainties.

We absolutely had no idea how the day was going to play out. Our focus was on trying to get back home. I had about three phone calls to make when we got back to Clarion. They all dealt with financial institutions and how if any of them could help us in our unique situation. All three phone calls provided no assistance therefore contributing to our still being stranded in Clarion, Pennsylvania. I had to laugh. It wasn't really a laughing matter because we actually were unable to go home. But what I thought might be three opportunities of help turned out to be shut windows of opportunity for us.

Lois and I knew God was with us, even guiding us through this situation as strange as it seemed. Revelation 3:7-8, "To the angel of the church in Philadelphia write: These are the words of Him who is holy and true, who holds the key of David. What He opens no one can shut, and what He shuts no one can open." These three financial opportunities were not what God was opening for us.

After arriving back in Clarion, we went to the garage and talked with Bob, the mechanic. I explained to Bob that I didn't have an answer yet about going home and I asked if we could hold on to the vehicle, he gave us to drive. Bob again showed us understanding and hospitality by allowing us the continual use of the vehicle we had been driving.

I told Bob that I was going to pay off my van so my brother's son-in-law, Rex, could drive from Howard to Clarion to haul our van back to Howard to dispose of it. Bob then offered to pay off our van and then he would fix it and use it to help other people as he had been helping us with the vehicle, he loaned us. I considered our van would be used in a type of ministry so I agreed to accept his offer of paying off the van. Bob paid Lois in cash in case we needed the money to get back home.

Lois called the motel and behold there was a room to rent. We were going to spend another day and night in Clarion. Let me say right now so there is no misunderstanding. Lois was missing work but we were not vacationing and sightseeing. We were literally stranded. We were earnestly trying to find a way to get home. This situation was for real and we had no idea how or why God was using this in our lives.

On Monday afternoon, Lois applied for a vehicle (we were desperate) with an online dealership and got approved to make a purchase. So, we spent all Monday afternoon, Monday evening, and early Tuesday morning trying to find a vehicle to purchase and have delivered to us. It had been a hope, when Lois was approved for a vehicle. As we settled in for the night we gave thanks to God for His guidance and provisions.

It was Tuesday morning, June 14, 2022 and our hope was that the uncertainties of Monday were behind us and that Tuesday would show us some hope of getting back home. We were earnestly searching for a vehicle. We were thinking that this was our possible way home. Find a vehicle we were interested in, purchase it, then have it delivered to us in Clarion. At 10:30 am I actually talked with someone from the online dealership. It was then I was informed that the online dealership delivers vehicles to your home, not where you are. That potential opportunity of hope just vanished like smoke disappearing in the air. Once again, I found myself laughing. I told Lois, "I could write a book about this week," though this week was just getting started.

We had one more turn in our road. Lois's phone was no longer working. She had an appointment to purchase a new cell phone. I stayed in the motel room with the dogs. By the way, we rented another night (Tuesday night) with the same motel we had been staying in. While Lois was busy getting her phone, I miraculously booked a Chrysler Pacifica rental minivan about an hour away from Clarion. I was elated that tomorrow we were going home! I was excited to tell Lois the news. I also had Lois stop by the garage and tell Bob, the mechanic, the news.

Even though we were now looking at going home the next day, I honestly couldn't make sense of why our days had been playing out as they had. I didn't know God's purpose and I wasn't understanding His ways. Such are experiencing the mysteries of God's leading. That night Lois and I praised God for His continual leading and His provisions. Make no mistake about it, our faith and patience were being tested and Bob, the mechanic, was watching.

CHAPTER TEN

Waiting

Wednesday morning, June 15, 2022, Lois and I woke up early. We left the motel with our dogs and drove the hour's drive to get the Chrysler Pacifica minivan that I had booked the day before. We wanted to get the rental van early because we would need to drive the one hour trip back to Clarion to transfer items from our van to the rental van and then start towards home.

At 8:05 am we walked into the car rental office where I had booked the minivan rental. I told the man behind the counter that I was there to get the Chrysler Pacifica minivan I had booked the day before. The man behind the counter told me I would have to wait till 12:00 noon because that was the turn in time for the vehicles that were rented out. We had gotten up early and drove an hour's drive only to be told we would have to wait another four hours before we could get the van. Welcome, Wednesday morning!

Then Lois asked the man behind the counter if we could at least start on the paperwork. He directed her to a young woman sitting behind a desk. The woman asked for our Pennsylvania driver's license and a major credit card.

Lois told her, "We don't have a Pennsylvania driver's license because we live in South Carolina and we don't have a major credit card either."

The young woman then replied to Lois, "If you don't have a Pennsylvania driver's license and a major credit card you cannot drive this vehicle."

Behold, another time, I laughed. It was like playing the game of Twister except whenever you would go to place your hand or foot on a colored spot, the spot would disappear.

We then made a phone call and discussed the situation with our son, Abe. Lois and I had no one from Pennsylvania to drive us home, nor did we have anyone to drive from South Carolina to Pennsylvania to take us home. The only other option was to see if we could purchase a vehicle from a dealership somewhere nearby.

We left the car rental agency and drove across the street and visited four car dealerships located side by side. If we had to purchase another vehicle then I wanted another Dodge Grand Caravan. I personally like this particular vehicle and I didn't want to settle for anything else. Need I say that neither of those four car dealerships had what I was looking for?

Lois drove us to a convenience store that was open for business but did not seem to have much business taking place. So, we parked for a period of time in a shady location because this was turning out to be a hot day for Pennsylvania standards and the vehicle Bob, the mechanic, loaned us had no air conditioning (yes, the windows were down for our dogs).

The day and a half that we looked for vehicles online, we saw a listing of a blue (Lois's favorite color) 2019 Dodge Grand Caravan (the particular type of vehicle I wanted) with a listing of only 39,000 miles. I called the dealership and talked with a salesman about our situation and the vehicle they had listed. This is when the day of "waiting" started for us.

We were waiting for the dealership to return our call as to our possible qualification for purchasing this particular vehicle. It was then the Holy Spirit brought a song to me for encouragement. The song describes the Christian believer waiting on God. But not just waiting on God but serving Him in obedience and worshiping Him through that period of waiting in confidence because He is faithful.

Again, I want to stress that we had no idea how the day was going to play out. We found ourselves waiting on God to lead us wherever, however, and whenever He chose for us. Anything to be done would be done through Him, and Him alone. The "waiting" was now testing our patience. Jesus spoke encouraging words to His disciples concerning their putting dependency on God, their heavenly Father.

Matthew 6:25-26, "Therefore, I tell you, do not worry about your life, what you will eat or drink; or about your body, what you will wear. Is not life more important than food, and the body more important than clothes? Look at the birds of the air; they do not sow or reap or store away in barns, and yet your heavenly Father feeds them. Are you not much more valuable than they?"

The dealership called us back and told us we were approved conditionally, meaning that we needed to provide certain paperwork for the full approval to happen. So, Lois and I called our daughter-in-law, Brittany, in South Carolina to look for a particular letter for me. My son and daughter-in-law own a gym in Beaufort, and Brittany was scheduled to go into the gym on this day but she stayed home instead. She therefore searched for and did find the letter I needed to give to the dealership. Brittany took a photograph of the letter using her cell phone and texted it to Lois's cell phone. The things that can be done with cell phones is remarkable.

It took us a little more than an hour to drive to the dealership and the day was getting warmer as time moved along. By the time we reached the dealership it was after lunchtime and getting right down hot. Wouldn't you know it, the dealership was dog friendly? That means our three dogs went into the nice air-conditioned dealership where we all spent the next few hours waiting for the approval process to play out. The dogs did really well in their behavior.

Waiting to see if we were going to be fully approved to purchase this 2019 Dodge Grand Caravan was a test of our faith and patience (I'll speak for myself, anyway). I didn't know what we would do if things didn't work out. I knew we were spending one more night (Wednesday) in the motel anyway. Along with the other days that we were stranded in Clarion, I knew today the Holy Spirit was at work in our lives adding to our spiritual character, faith and patience.

All that God does in our lives as Christian believers is always to our benefit and to His glory. James 1:12, "Blessed is the man who perseveres under trial, because when he has stood the test, he will receive the crown of life that God has promised to those who love Him." The Apostle Paul puts it in a different perspective but equally encouraging. Romans 8:18, "I consider that our present sufferings are not worth comparing with the glory that will be revealed in us." All that God accomplishes in our lives will last for eternity.

Finally, the news was delivered to us that we were fully approved for the purchasing of the blue 2019 Dodge Grand Caravan. We knew that the next day we were finally going home. We didn't leave the dealership until approximately 7:45 pm. According to Google we had 90 miles to drive and about two hours of driving ahead of us.

Lois took the lead since she was utilizing GPS (again) and I followed her in the van we just purchased. We pulled into the motel parking lot about 10:00 pm.

But as we pulled into the parking lot of the motel I heard a sound I was familiar with but was hoping wasn't so. It sounded as though there was a problem with the brakes on the van. I would have Bob, the mechanic, check the brakes in the morning. In settling in for the night I told Lois at the end of a very long day of waiting, "My faith and patience was much tested today and I wouldn't give myself an A.

Very quickly God's Holy Spirit reminded me that I didn't give myself the test today, God did, and therefore, I am not the one doing the grading, God is. Lois and I thanked God for not only bringing us through this trying day but provided us with a newer vehicle to drive home the next day.

CHAPTER ELEVEN

Homeward Bound

It was Thursday, June 16, 2022, and Lois and I were up early. Today was the day we were finally going home. We had been stranded in Clarion, Pennsylvania for five days and we wanted to get started as soon as possible. So, we had our breakfast and packed everything we had, including our dogs. Lois then checked us out of the motel.

When we arrived at the garage I asked Bob, the mechanic, to listen to the brakes and then look at them. No doubt about it, one of the rear brakes was worn down to nothing. I did not want to drive anywhere with the brakes in that condition so I asked Bob to put new rear brakes on our newly purchased van. While Bob was putting the new brakes on the van, I called the dealership and complained. The used car manager apologized and said they would reimburse us for the cost of the new brakes and having them put on.

I had a final talk with Bob who had told Lois and I that he and his wife were driving to Georgia around the fourth of July holiday to visit his niece.

"That's great!" I replied to Bob.

So, I asked Bob for his niece's name again so our church could be praying for her. I then had a closing conversation with Bob as once more I had the opportunity to share God's love for him.

I said, "Bob, I want to thank you for offering to help us with the use of this vehicle, though, if we hadn't accepted your offer, it would not have benefitted us." I went on to say, "Likewise, God makes His plan of salvation available to us as sinners through His Son, Jesus Christ, but if we as sinners don't take Him up on His offer, it then does not benefit us," I continued by saying, "Bob, I believe God chose to work through you so He could minister to us and bless us."

I then told Bob, "Because you allowed God to work through you to our benefit, I am going to pray for God to bless you and your garage." "And He will do it, somehow," I told Bob. I then prayed, "Father, I ask you to bless Bob and his garage for his service to you in ministering unto and blessing Lois and I. Amen!" Both Lois and Bob said Amen as well.

As Lois paid the bill for the new brakes, I shook hands with Bob and said, "Bob, I don't think of you as a mere business acquaintance but a friend. And if you come to faith In Jesus then we'll be spiritual brothers." With that, Lois and I and our

dogs drove up the street to Burger King for lunch.
After a quick lunch we were finally homeward
bound.

The Christian believer, those who have put
faith in God and His Son, Jesus Christ, are
spiritually homeward bound. Just like Clarion,
Pennsylvania was not our home, neither is this
world the home of the Christian believer. The
Apostle Paul speaks of the Christian believer's
citizenship as being in heaven. Philippians
3:20, "But our citizenship is in heaven. And we
eagerly await a Savior from there, the Lord Jesus
Christ, who by the power that enables Him to bring
everything under His control, will transform our lowly
bodies so that they will be like His glorious body."

Lois and I both grew up in the state of
Pennsylvania. But in due time we moved to South
Carolina of which we are now citizens. The Apostle
Paul states that the Christian believer once was a
citizen of this world because of our sin and following
the ways of Satan. Ephesians 2:1-5, "As for you,
you were dead in your transgressions and sins, in
which you used to live when you followed the ways
of this world and of the ruler of the kingdom of the
air, the spirit who is now at work in those who are
disobedient. All of us also lived among them at one
time, gratifying the cravings of our sinful nature and
following its desires and thoughts.

Like the rest, we were by nature objects of
wrath. But because of His great love for us, God,
who is rich in mercy, made us alive with Christ even

when we were dead in transgressions—it is by grace you have been saved." Even before the Apostle Paul spoke these words, the Lord Jesus Christ told His disciples similar words. John 15:18-19, "If the world hates you, keep in mind that it hated me first. If you belonged to the world, it would love you as its own. As it is, you do not belong to the world, but I have chosen you out of the world. That is why the world hates you."

Lois drove west on I-80 then on to I-79 south that took us into the state of West Virginia. At the West Virginia Welcome Center, I then took over the driving. We continued on I-79 south through many valleys within the mountains of West Virginia. There were many high bridges that we crossed, some over rivers though many were not. When I reached I-19, I followed it southwest which took us to a road I was very familiar with, I-77 south. I-77 south would take us all the way to Columbia, South Carolina.

Each time I entered a new state on the way home I would send everyone in our church a "Welcome to," so everyone was aware of our progress. Lois and I were so looking forward to getting back home. By this time, I felt led by the Holy Spirit to write a book about our trip. So, on the long drive home Lois and I rehashed our trip, especially our stranded stay in Clarion, Pennsylvania. Lois and I talked about minute details how God was working in our situations and ultimately our lives. Surely, I believed many could identify with the title of the book, "So, You Had A Tough Week, Huh?"

It was about 9:30 pm on Thursday night and Lois was driving us through the Charlotte, North Carolina area when I sent Bob a text about something I had forgotten to tell him. Bob texted me back informing me that a tornado hit his home area about 6:30 pm. I asked if there was any damage and he replied there were many trees down and the electric power was out.

A few minutes later I texted Bob, "Welcome to South Carolina." Bob texted back, "Still praying U make it…it has been a trying week…God bless…" Lois and I believed God had been revealing Himself to Bob all week long and speaking to Bob's heart as well. Surely Bob knew what Lois and I went through because we kept him informed daily. We finally got home approaching 1:30 am Friday morning. Finally, we were home. I thought of Dorothy, on the Wizard of Oz, and her chanting words, "There's no place like home, there's no place like home."

As I was jotting notes for this book on Saturday morning June 18, 2022, I was thinking of calling Bob and telling him to be watchful for God's blessings on him. Almost immediately God's Holy Spirit told me that He had blessed Bob on Thursday night when the tornado hit his property.

About 11:00 am Saturday morning I called Bob who was at the garage. I said, "Bob, I thought about calling you to encourage you to be watchful of how God might bless you." I then went on to say,

"Almost immediately God's Holy Spirit told me that He blessed you with protection when the tornado hit your property. Trees came down and you lost electrical power but no trees fell on your house. Besides that, God answered the prayer of blessing you that I prayed Thursday morning. God is revealing Himself to you Bob." With that we said our goodbyes and Bob encouraged me to keep in touch with him.

CHAPTER TWELVE

For His Glory

The Bible is full of stories about the servants of God who lived by faith. In fact, Hebrews chapter 11 in the Bible can be called The Faith Hall of Fame chapter. There are many whose names are shared as well as a brief testimony of their acts of faith. In reality this is a short list of those who could be considered God's Faith Hall of Famers because of their faith they expressed in God.

The Apostle Paul states in Romans 8:14, "Because those who are led by the Spirit of God are sons of God." By faith I say that the story you have read in this book, besides being a true story, is a God story. God Himself, brought this whole story about. I did not know Lois and I would be part of a story God was going to bring about through real life circumstances in our lives. But as I said in the introduction of the book, Lois and I have lived many years living life in the Spirit and that takes place by the virtue of faith.

And God has been developing that faith in our lives ever since we made that first step of faith in Him as we each prayed to Him many years ago, "Dear Jesus, I confess I am a sinner and I believe you died for my sins. I repent of my sins and I ask you to forgive me and cleanse me of all my sins. May you come into my life and live in me as Savior and Lord of my life. In Jesus name I pray. Amen!"

To tell you the truth, it wasn't until Sunday morning of June 12, 2022, during my conversation with Bob, the mechanic, that through the eyes of faith I saw that our vehicle breakdown was a God thing, all for the purpose of meeting Bob. Now I know that for many of you who are reading this might find that statement hard to understand or believe, but there are many Christian believers because of their own life in the Spirit can truly understand such a statement.

Throughout eternity God has been doing things that mortal man could never believe if it were not for the faith, He gives them that enables them to believe. All of those individuals listed in Hebrews chapter eleven with their great feats of faith are listed so as to encourage all who read of them to come to faith in God themselves. But it was God who enabled each one of them to do what they did. To God alone goes the glory.

Servants of God, whomever they were, whomever they are, and whomever they will be, are to be reminded that it was God and is God working in their lives to accomplish what they accomplished or will accomplish. The Apostle Paul speaks of this in 1 Corinthians 1:26-31, "Brothers, think of what you were when you were called. Not many of you were wise by human standards, not many were influential; not many were of noble birth. But God chose the foolish things of the world to shame the wise; God chose the weak things of the world to shame the strong. He chose the lowly things of the world and the despised things–and the things that are not–to nullify the things that are, so that no one may boast before Him.

It is because of Him that you are in Christ Jesus, who has become for us wisdom from God– that is, our righteousness, holiness and redemption. Therefore, as it is written: Let him who boasts boast in the Lord."

It was God who chose Lois and I to go to Pennsylvania and witness to one whom God has been pursuing for many years because of His exceeding love for the unsaved. It was God who chose to place us in a position of being "stranded" so that He might test our faith and patience. It was God's plan and for His purpose that He would lead us into service to Him for which Lois and I are honored to have served Him. God guided us each day by His Spirit and by faith, always providing us with what we needed while keeping us in the place of needing Him. We give God the glory!

I encourage fellow Christian believers to exercise faith and ask God to reveal Himself to you as you find yourself in trying situations and circumstances. It very well may be that God has chosen that situation to work in you and through you for His purposes. God really does not want you wandering in the darkness of your situations and dilemmas. Heed God's words that He spoke through the prophet Jeremiah. Jeremiah 29:12-13, "Then you will call upon me and come and pray to me, and I will listen to you. You will seek me and find me when you seek me with all your heart."

If you are a reader who has not yet come to faith in God and His Son, Jesus Christ, I encourage you to listen to the words of the Apostle Peter. 2 Peter 3:9, "The Lord is not slow in keeping His promise, as some understand slowness. He is patient with you, not wanting anyone to perish, but everyone to come to repentance."

The Apostle Paul speaks the most encouraging words of not allowing time to rob you of the opportunity to take that first step of faith in God and His Son, Jesus Christ. 2 Corinthians 6:2 "For He says, 'In the time of my favor I heard you, and in the day of salvation I helped you.' I tell you now is the time of God's favor, now is the day of salvation."

In closing, I thank you for riding along with Lois and I on our trip to Pennsylvania. I hope God revealed Himself to you as He did to us. God tested our faith and patience but then He gave growth to both of those areas in each of our lives. So, if you should find yourself in some unexplainable situation and a surprising one at that, it may very well be that you are Experiencing the Mysteries of God's Leading.

APPENDIX

Benediction

I completed the writing of this book in two weeks. My hope was to write it and get it published so that my brother, Tim, would be able to read it. But sadly, that was not to be. My brother, Tim, died on Sunday morning of July 10, 2022.

With the passing of my brother came a pause in sending this book to the publisher. It was a pause the Holy Spirit brought about so He could give me this benediction to the book.

Tim's body was available for viewing by family members on Monday, July 11, 2022. Tim's body was then cremated and a Memorial Service was held for Tim on Wednesday, July 12, 2022. Tim knew he was going to die and that his life was coming to its end. He knew there would be a memorial service for him so he planned it as he wanted it to take place.

At a memorial service the deceased person is the one being acknowledged, recognized, and remembered. But for Tim, as any Christian believer, it is God who ultimately is acknowledged, recognized, and remembered. For it is God who planned Tim's entire life from beginning to end, even before anything He created. Ephesians 1:4-6, "For He chose us in Him before the creation of the world to be holy and blameless in His sight. In love He predestined us to be adopted as His sons through Jesus Christ, in accordance with His pleasure and will—to the praise of His glorious grace, which He has freely given us in the One He loves."

God knew Tim, as He knows everyone before they are born. Jeremiah 1:5a, "Before I formed you in the womb I knew you, before you were born, I set you apart."

Everyone's lifespan is known by God because they are determined by God. Job 14:5, "Man's days are determined; you have decreed the number of his months and have set limits he cannot exceed."

As for Tim, as all Christian believers can, reflected in his life the blessings of God upon his life. The Psalmist characterizes the life of the godly person in Psalm 1:1-3, "Blessed is the man who does not walk in the counsel of the wicked or stand in the way of sinners or sit in the seat of mockers. But his delight is in the law of the Lord, and on His law, he meditates day and night. He is like a tree planted by streams of water, which yields its fruit in season and whose leaf does not wither. Whatever he does prospers."

Life is sometimes long, yet short for others. It is God who decrees the number of our days. But it is the choice of every individual how they will live their life. One can live their life in God or apart from God, each one makes that choice. For Tim, he made the choice for God.

Since God is Spirit we do not see him with our physical eyes. But because He lives in the life of the Christian believer Tim experienced "life in the Spirit." Though much of Tim's life was known by those who had a relationship with him and therefore knew him somewhat, yet it is God alone who knows him completely. I say that in present tense because Tim was given the gift of eternal life the moment he accepted God's salvation and Jesus came into his life. Tim is still alive in the presence of his heavenly Father and his Lord and Savior, Jesus Christ.

Even as Tim's liver disease put him on the end of the road of his life, God was with him, preparing him for departing this life to go "home" to the Father. Even in his sickness he could understand the words of the Apostle Paul in Romans 8:14, "If we live, we live to the Lord; and if we die, we die to the Lord. So, whether we live or die, we belong to the Lord."

From the time Tim received the salvation of God by placing his faith in Jesus Christ until his death, the Holy Spirit was continually at work conforming Tim into the image (character) of his

Savior. Therefore, the words the Apostle Paul spoke to the Philippian church could apply to Tim as well. Philippians 1:6, "Being confident of this, that He who began a good work in you will carry it on to completion until the day of Christ Jesus."

Because of the fellowship and ministry Tim had with the Holy Spirit in his life, at the end Tim could express the words of the Apostle Paul in 2 Timothy 4:7-8, "I have fought the good fight, I have finished the race, I have kept the faith. Now there is in store for me the crown of righteousness, which the Lord, the righteous judge, will award to me on that day—and not only to me, but also to all who have longed for His appearing."

Early Sunday morning of July 10, 2022, by the ministry of the Holy Spirit and in privacy the Lord Jesus Christ spoke the words to Tim which 2000 years ago He spoke to the thief on the cross, "I tell you the truth, today you will be with me in paradise" (Luke 23:43). God's holy angels carried his spirit to his eternal heavenly home where he now lives in the presence of his heavenly Father and his Lord and Savior, Jesus Christ.

For all those who will miss Tim, there is the joy of knowing that if you are a Christian believer, you will see Tim again. 1 Thessalonians 4:16-17, "For the Lord Himself will come down from heaven, with a loud command, with the voice of the archangel and with the trumpet call of God, and the dead in Christ will rise first. After that, we who are still alive and are left will be caught up together with them in the clouds to meet the Lord in the air. And so, we will be with the Lord forever."

Jude 24-25, "To Him who is able to keep you from falling and to present you before His glorious presence without fault and with great joy—to the only God our Savior be glory, majesty, power and authority, through Jesus Christ our Lord, before all ages, now and forevermore! Amen."